RAISE YOUR Ebenezer

A STEP-BY-STEP GUIDE TO
Map Your Walk with God

KIT KENZIE

WESTBOW
PRESS®
A DIVISION OF THOMAS NELSON
& ZONDERVAN

WestBow Press books may be ordered through booksellers or by contacting:

WestBow Press
A Division of Thomas Nelson & Zondervan
1663 Liberty Drive
Bloomington, IN 47403
www.westbowpress.com
844-714-3454

ISBN: 979-8-3850-1073-8 (sc)
ISBN: 979-8-3850-1074-5 (e)

Library of Congress Control Number: 2023920943

Print information available on the last page.

WestBow Press rev. date: 02/07/2024

DEDICATION

To my pastor and his wife,
you are two of my Ebenezers.

To my children and grandchildren,
you were the reason I finished this book.
I love you so much and
I hope you will always follow Jesus.
You are His legacy.

PREFACE

What's the Deal with This Title?

When I first heard the word *Ebenezer,* I was nine years old and it was snowing outside. I was watching TV and hiding my eyes from the cold-hearted miser who despised Christmas. Ebenezer Scrooge was living every day in fear for his soul. He scared me. I was in my midfifties, sitting in church, and I knew our pastor must have made a mistake. *Ebenezer Scrooge in church? Wait. What?* He made reference to how the word *Ebenezer* was used in a verse from a beautiful, old hymn "Come Thou Fount." *I've sung this hymn a thousand times.* My thoughts stammered. *What is he talking about? Forget the meaning,* I thought as I tore open my hymnal. *Where is that verse?*

> Here I raise my Ebenezer
> Hither by thy help I've come.
> And I hope, by thy good pleasure
> Safely to arrive at home.
> (Robert Robinson)

There it was, just like our pastor said. So with Scrooge out of the picture, I sat up a little taller and listened a little more closely, hoping I hadn't missed the meaning. He explained that after rebelling and complaining against God, over and over again, the Israelites acquired the ark of the covenant. Because of this, they thought they were safe from any enemies that might come their way. Later on in 1 Samuel 7 of the Old Testament, the prophet Samuel and the Israelites found themselves under attack by the Philistines. Fearing for their lives, the Israelites begged Samuel to pray for them in their imminent battle with these barbarians. He then offered a sacrifice to God and prayed for their protection. Samuel's prayer was heard by God. As a result of God's intervention, the Philistines lost the fight and retreated. Scripture records, "Then Samuel took a stone and set it up between Mizpah and Shen, and called it Ebenezer, saying, 'Thus far The Lord has helped us'" (1 Samuel 7:12). This was an unimaginable and profound answer to prayer!

By definition, *Ebenezer* simply means "stone of help." It is a memorial set up to proclaim not only where the enemy was crushed but also to recognize the great help that God had given to the one raising the stone.

This rattled my whole being. I was taken with this new word and its meaning for my life. *I have Ebenezers,* I almost exclaimed in church! Immediately my mind reeled, recalling instances in my life when God helped me. I was so excited that I began writing them down all over the sermon notes.

I remember thinking, *The God of the universe has given me a lifetime of Ebenezers—proof, evidence—that He loves me and that I can always trust Him.* This was the coolest thing I could imagine.

I knew what I had to do next. I set out to map my own personal Ebenezers by listing all the ways God helped me through struggles, pain, and suffering (my victories from God). The Lord's hand was all over my life. A new sense of purpose and knowledge of His faithfulness began filling me. I started writing a memoir that gradually evolved into what you are reading today.

So that's just what this project became—a testament of my simple, little, amazing, redeemed life to help build my trust and ultimately glorify Him. I wanted others to have this experience as well so this guidebook was created just for you! It will allow you to map your walk with God and discover your own Ebenezers.

I was so thrilled when our pastor's wife suggested we use this mapping process for our Ladies' Retreat! My excitement quickly turned into anxiety. Yet by the grace of God, despite a few major difficulties, the retreat was a great success for all twenty-eight of us who attended. Moreover, although I did not anticipate it, this event quickly became yet another personal Ebenezer.

Your life is a God story too. This guidebook serves as a tool to help you remember and plot your own Ebenezers. As you witness the goodness of God in your life, He receives the glory and your faith grows. You will be able to look back with eyes of faith and see that He was there with you all along in your blessings and battles alike.

After creating my own map, with the final product in my hands, I was just awestruck by the work God had accomplished. All I could think was *I really can trust Him with every detail of my life.* I am so excited for you to get started!

INTRODUCTION

So you've bought this book and taken a chance on me, a grandma and new author. You need to know a few more things. I was an A student in high school and was awarded "Woman of the Year" at graduation. Political science was my choice of college study just because it seemed interesting and easy. I worked as a police officer, prison guard, and investigator early in my career. I ran for political office and was elected. Later on, I went back to school to become a teacher, and further down the road, I started my own storytelling business. To God be the glory for using all these scraps.

Now before you start thinking, *What a compelling, exciting life she's had,* you also need to know that I've broken all Ten Commandments, and I know that you know adultery and murder are two of them.

THE REVEALING

While I was in college and interning as a police officer, I met Bob at a party. We dated, we engaged in premarital sex, I got pregnant, I had an abortion, and then we got married. A few years later, while working in a prison, I began a relationship with a coworker. Bob found out. This was a time of profound confusion and grief for both of us, but then Bob decided he wanted part of the action so we agreed to have an open marriage.

Thankfully, after living in utter chaos and sadness, this promiscuous lifestyle fizzled out shortly thereafter and we got back on track. Bob and I wanted to start over and have a baby. I got pregnant and life was wonderful, until I found out that he had another girlfriend. He moved out, assisted by the toe of my boot, and within a year, we were divorced. I gave birth to our baby boy, Curtis. All that drama in six years—really bad stuff, not glamorous at all, but part of my history nonetheless.

It's my privilege to share that my story is a story of redemption as well. I was raised Catholic and went to a Catholic high school. I knew the tenets of Christianity but sadly didn't know much about Christ or what it meant to be a Christian. I had never really heard the Gospel outright. It was only friendly background noise among other and more persuasive voices. I knew no Christian jargon, not many books of the Bible, or what a Christian lifestyle meant. I only tell you this for context because of what happened next.

I had been divorced a year, enjoying my freedom with my newfound boyfriend. We were sleeping in bed and two-year-old Curtis was down the hall asleep in his room. I had a dream. Jesus appeared to me in the upper left-hand corner of the room and clearly spoke. *"Move away from sin, come follow Me, and sing My praises."*

I was simply overtaken by a feeling of love and belonging. I felt that no matter what the cost, I had to go with Him. I remember thinking, *I would leave my son, my house, my money.* I just felt so compelled to go that nothing else mattered. And then God whispered, *"I have just shown you a glimpse of My glory."* There was no mistaking that I was going to say yes to Jesus. I did, and my life changed forever in that moment.

I woke up and saw my boyfriend's head on the pillow. I shook him, and then I told him he had to leave and I would explain later. In my mind, all I could think was *I have just been saved by Jesus Christ.* Whatever that meant, I hadn't a clue, but I knew that I had to get back to church and find out. Jesus met me at the front door. I wept as I told Him I reeked of sin and offered my repentance. I gave Him all my filthy rags from the past. In exchange, He clothed me in His righteousness. I was forgiven, I was made new, and Jesus has been my Savior ever since.

Please know that even after my repentance, it took a long time for me to be able to talk about my past. At first, I disguised my story as I told it. Even as a new believer, it always began with me being the victim of an unfaithful husband while I carried his baby. It wasn't until a few years ago, while I was writing this book, that I was convicted to retell my story including the truth of my own adultery in the early days of marriage.

Fast-forward seven years. I was teaching high school and met a Christian man. We were married and had a daughter, Ruthie. I paused my teaching career to stay home with my children, but it turned out to be much longer than I had planned. For years, yes, years, I spent time in a dark bedroom with migraines and clinical depression. At one point, I was even hospitalized. God didn't answer when I cried out to Him so I quit praying. It was as though He was totally shutting me out and I began to doubt His goodness. I lost my trust in Him for a long time, but God was faithful to me once again. He pulled me out of unbearable circumstances and directed me to prayer, counseling, medication and exercise.

ENCOURAGEMENT

I hope you can see that my story is one of candid sinfulness, long-suffering, and blessings from the Lord. It mirrors the relationship between God and His people. They disobey, God convicts, they cry out to Him, and He helps and restores them. And the cycle continues—a simple but difficult up and down trajectory. In my experience, everyone's life pretty much runs this same course, to a greater or lesser degree. This will be crucial to remember as you start thinking about your own life.

I've always been rather introspective about my life's highs and lows, but more so after I became a believer. I struggled daily to trust God with my future. I always felt like the next bad thing was waiting just around the corner. *What do I do when the next shoe drops?* So just as I eventually did, you need to be honest with yourself, in essence honest with God, as you work on your map. By grace, He did not come to condemn you; He came to save you.

While writing this book, I stumbled upon a Bible verse. (How many times has that happened?) "Let the redeemed of the Lord tell their story" (Psalm 107:2). This is a call to declare the mighty works of God, not just from scripture but from our own life. Your story is evidence of a good and faithful God, and He is urging you to tell it.

You may still be thinking, *My life is average at best.* Stop! As a believer in Christ, you have a foreordained, apple of God's eye story inside you. I'll say it another way. You have a predetermined honored place in history. *Did you catch that?* You were included in His grand story before you were even born. This means the story of your life has been included in His bigger plan of redemption before the beginning of time. The conclusion? Your life story has meaning and purpose.

Repeat after me. *"My story is epic!"* Not only is it epic, but you are also called to share it.

> Give praise to the Lord, proclaim his name; make known among the nations what he has done. Sing to him, sing praises to him; tell of all his wondrous acts. (Psalm 105:1–2)

THE MAPPING PROCESS

First and foremost, He allowed your physical life to begin-your birth, your first Ebenezer!

> For you created my inmost being,
> you knit me together in my mother's womb.
> I praise you because I am fearfully and wonderfully made:
> your works are wonderful.
> I know that full well.
> My frame was not hidden from you
> when I was made in the secret place,
> when I was woven together in the depths of the earth.
> Your eyes saw my unformed body;
> All the days ordained for me were written in your book
> before one of them came to be. (Psalm 139:13–16)

This is where your story starts, and it will be the first entry on your map. Like your birth, some other Ebenezers will also be easy to recognize, such as when you became a believer.

Before we continue, however, let's make sure you understand exactly what an Ebenezer is and what I'm asking you to record. As you look back over your life, I want you to try to remember the times in the past when the Lord blessed you or helped you. Maybe against the odds, maybe seemingly impossible odds, He gave you a victory. Try to recall God's past faithfulness to you, where He unexpectedly did something amazing. Remember no one can tell you what amazing is or what your Ebenezers are.

Begin by asking yourself these questions: Where and when did He teach me something? Did He answer a prayer? Provide clarity? You may have hit the end of a road and God showed up. Was there a defining moment? A blessing? Where did God bring life out of a broken thing? Where did He intervene and take action? I think it will help if I give you a few examples from my own life.

Growing up, I was never interested in staying overnight at friends' houses—that is, until I met Chrissy. In seventh grade, we clicked. We had the same interests, had the same sense of humor—you get the picture. I immediately asked my mother if I could stay over when the invitation came.

The minute I walked into Chrissy's house, I knew something was different. First of all, there wasn't a beer can in sight and her father was very engaging. His smile couldn't have been brighter. Chrissy's mom brought dinner to the table and everyone sat and reached for each other's hands. *What's this?* A prayer of thanks was poetically spoken, and the sibling banter began. Her brothers and sisters laughed and teased and were kind to each other. I was mesmerized.

You see, my family was the opposite. I had an alcoholic father and a working mother who was struggling to make ends meet with six children. After this sleepover with Chrissy, my heart had been pierced. I wanted a family like hers. More importantly, I instinctively knew I needed it. That visit eventually became one of the early Ebenezers on my map for two reasons. First, it touched me deeply and I couldn't shake it. Second, I found out much later in life that her family members were believers and they had prayed for me throughout the years, even when we had lost touch. God also gave me the gift of being able to reconnect with Chrissy and her family when we were in our fifties. I couldn't wait to share with them how their actions of that night affected my life forever. This is just one example of how a simple childhood reflection can turn into an Ebenezer.

One other brief example is I played sports all through my childhood and high school years. Later in life, I would bike, run, and swim. I had a membership at a college where I would swim when I was able to get a lane, hit or miss. I needed this outlet for my physical and mental health. This continued for years until COVID hit in 2020, bringing everything to a standstill, including me when I got it in May 2021. I felt lost and asked the Lord to please fill this very important void in my life.

I remembered that our local school was supposed to build a new pool! The project was going well and the pool was supposed to open in September of that same year. When the time came, I called right away to see when the public swim hours were scheduled. I was told there would be no public swim hours for the unforeseen future. I was heartbroken. One week later, I got a call from the school informing me that the pool was going to be open to the public immediately and that I could reserve a lane for three days a week at no cost. The school is only two miles away from my house. I was floored, humbled, and so thankful to God. I understand that this may not seem "Ebenezer-worthy" to some, but for me, it was huge and God knew it. He always does immeasurably more than we ask, and this was a perfect example. I used this illustration to show you that Ebenezer choices will be so different for everyone. Praise God. He knows just what we need, when we need it.

Some Ebenezers will clearly jump out at you. I've already mentioned two and they are the two most significant days of your life–the day you were born and the day you said yes to Jesus. You probably will also choose some of the most fulfilling days of your life: first job, graduation, marriage, or having a baby. What occurred to me as I thought about my own Ebenezers was that most of them were tied to trials. I had made some sinful choices; others were simply struggles that God allowed for my sanctification and His glory.

In the third verse of that hymn, "Come Thou Fount," which I hope becomes "our song," it states,

> Prone to wander Lord, I feel it.
> Prone to leave the God I love ...

We are all prone to wander. We all stroll around in the arenas of temptation because that is our default setting—our sinful nature. I groan as I tell you that sin is here to stay and will reside in us until we are with Christ. Yet God is faithful. That's His nature. Your map will allow you to see how He used every tattered fray of your meandering and gave you the strength to overcome and raise high your Ebenezers. Here's your chance. Go ahead and glorify Him! "Declare his glory among the nations, his marvelous deeds among the peoples" (1 Chronicles 16:24).

"We will tell the next generation the praiseworthy deeds of the Lord, His power and the wonders he has done" (Psalm 78:4).

I'm sure that some of these trials you'd rather forget, or maybe you have actually just forgotten. It may be painful to relive these storms, but please don't hold back. God was in charge of these storms. My friend stated it best when she said, "If you don't include your hardships, it cheapens the Ebenezers." And remember, this is *your* map and for your eyes only. If you're still struggling with this aspect of the project, do what I did. Use a code! My adultery became the huge, red letter "A!" (You can laugh. It's OK.) You can also decide to change the names, dates, or whatever—as long as *you* understand it.

Now I know right now, if not before, your heart is racing. The anxiety is rising and you still may be a bit confused or at least have some reservations or questions. That's normal. It will become clearer. Trust me. No, I take that back. Trust God and take a breath.

INSTRUCTIONS

Let's get started organizing your life! As a teenage girl, or maybe even now, did you ever take any of those little quizzes in magazines or online meant to reveal some new, amazing personality trait that would change your life? You might have discovered what fashion style or color suited you best, what sort of man you should marry, or what side of your brain was dominant. The questions were short, fun, and intriguing. That's just how you are going to get started finding your Ebenezers. Your quizzes are called "Inspiration Pages" (IPs) and are located in the back of the book. The goal of these sheets is to help you remember the high and low events in your past.

Here is a sampling of what you can expect:

- Early age ordering sheets
- High school
- College
- Top ten influencers in my life
- Three best/worst things that ever happened to me
- Romantic interests/significant friends
- Singleness/marriage/family/addresses/jobs
- Private page
- God in your life/your testimony
- Ordering charts: general time period/decades, etc.
- Map template sheets
- Author examples

You can start with any of the IPs or use any other tools that work for you. If it's easier for you to do a complete "brain dump" and/or simply journal your life, go for it. It's your story and your map. It doesn't matter how you get there. The end goal is simple to see God's goodness in your life! Hang with me. I have a few more "life-saving" recommendations before you begin.

1. Prayer journals and/or resumes can help reveal Ebenezers.
2. Familiarize yourself with the "Inspiration Pages."
3. Think God moments.
4. Take breaks.
5. When the juices flow, keep writing.
6. After completion of the IPs, highlight Ebenezers and struggles. (Choose two colors.)
7. Put events in order by numbering on IPs or use charts provided.
8. Start mapping on templates provided.

Don't get hung up on dates. This was a real concern for the women on the retreat. They were afraid of not getting the right order or not remembering exact details. God will bring to mind what you are supposed to remember, and He's not overly picky about the order!

I do want to emphasize that it actually works to set the IPs aside now and again—maybe for days. It may sound cliche, but use this time to pray and hang out with God. Everyone thinks this is a good idea, *but does anyone really do it?* Here's your chance. Talk to Him about going back in time. Ask Him to help you remember what He did for you. This is not wasted time; it will bless you and glorify Him.

Don't overthink your map. Sometimes I couldn't decide whether something was actually an Ebenezer or not but still wanted to include it. In this case, use the lines between the Ebenezers to record these extra details. I have provided two personal pages from my own map for you to view at the very end of the IPs. Remember, my map began as an outline for a **memoir** before it was a part of this guidebook. It kept getting longer as God revealed Himself to me. Hallelujah! Map length and details are only important if they are important to you. Feel free to cut out completed map pages and then tape together.

In closing, I want to remind you of what you are actually mapping. It's *God's story of you,* one of His children He called by name. Your map is a journey with the

Almighty. As a matter of fact, He is the real author, not you. And please remember that on this side of heaven, our perspective will always be impaired, but God will reveal what He needs you to see. You are actually drawing your promised transformation by God—the process of your sanctification! What a rush! I pray that you can relax, relish this adventure, and be intentional in finishing your map. I hope when you look at your map you are filled with the "peace that passes all understanding" and will put one foot in front of the other to see what He *does* have around the next corner. I am praying for you! Godspeed!

INSPIRATION PAGES

"Let the redeemed of the Lord tell their story"

— PSALM 107:2

Ages 0-10

I was born to _____ father

_____ mother

Describe Dad _____

Describe Mom _____

Step parents? Yes/No
Describe them _____

My birthdate/place _____

Any details/description about your birth? _____

My hometown/s _____

Did your parents work? Yes/No

Where _____

Grandparents _____

Describe them _____

_____

Ages 0-10 continued

Any siblings? Yes/No

Describe them _____

_____

Adults I was close to outside of my immediate family

_____

_____

Elementary School(s) attended _____

Fun stuff I did (activities, hobbies, sports, etc)

_____

_____

Places I lived _____

_____

A wonderful memory

_____

An embarrassing moment

_____

A very sad situation

_____

Anything else?

_____

Ages 10-14

I lived _____

School(s) I attended

_____

Best friends and why _____

_____

Favorite teacher(s) and why _____

_____

My homelife

_____

_____

Places I visited

_____

_____

_____

_____

Ages 10-14 continued

New interests

_____

_____

_____

This happened to me and it stands out

_____

_____

_____

Anything else?

_____

_____

_____

HIGH SCHOOL
Ages 15-18

For better or worse, think significance. List names of friends, teachers, trips, teams, hobbies, clubs and youth groups. Think of your favorite things to do, dreaded subjects, embarrassing moments—all those things that make up each year.

FRESHMAN YEAR

_____

_____

SOPHOMORE YEAR

_____

_____

JUNIOR YEAR

_____

_____

SENIOR YEAR

_____

_____

HIGH SCHOOL continued

Family situations

_____

_____

_____

Church

_____

_____

_____

Anything else?

_____

_____

_____

COLLEGE

Freshman Year:

When? _____

Where? _____

Coursework: _____

Sophomore Year:

When? _____

Where? _____

Coursework: _____

Junior Year:

When? _____

Where?_____

Coursework:_____

Anything amazing or downright awful?

_____

_____

COLLEGE continued

SENIOR YEAR

Major _____

Internship _____

Friendships _____

Boyfriends/Fiance _____

Job Offers _____

Rejections _____

Highlights _____

Disappointments _____

Moved _____

What was happening at home? _____

SPECIAL RELATIONSHIPS

Early Romantic Interests

Names and thoughts

_____

_____

_____

_____

_____

_____

Significant friendships along the way

_____

_____

_____

_____

_____

_____

PLACES I'VE LIVED

(try to put in order)

_____

_____

_____

_____

_____

JOBS/VOLUNTEERING

(try to put them in order)

_____

_____

_____

_____

_____

MY TOP TEN INFLUENTIAL PEOPLE

(positively or negatively, not necessarily in any order)

1. _____

_____

2. _____

_____

3. _____

_____

4. _____

_____

5. _____

_____

6. _____

_____

7. _____

_____

8. _____

_____

9. _____

_____

10. _____

_____

WOW! MOMENTS

The THREE BEST THINGS that ever happened to me, not including my salvation, my marriage or children.

(and you thought this would be easy)

1. _____

2. _____

3. _____

The THREE WORST THINGS (or more) that ever happened to me.

1. _____

2. _____

3. _____

4. _____

MY MARRIAGE

Spouse's Name _____

When and how we met

_____

_____

His special qualities

_____

_____

Struggles

_____

_____

Where we are today

_____

_____

MORE THAN ONE MARRIAGE

(things I remember most about my divorce(s) or widowhood)

What I remember most about my divorce(s) or widowhood:

I remarried _____ when I was_____

(name)   (age)

Blended?

_____

_____

Visitations?

_____

_____

Struggles?

_____

_____

Early years?

_____

_____

Then what?

_____

_____

STAGES OF SINGLENESS

Have you always been single? Yes/No

Thoughts

_____

_____

Do you enjoy being single? Yes/No

(mind your own business!)

_____

_____

_____

_____

Elaborate

_____

_____

Have your feelings changed over time? Yes/No

_____

_____

How do you spend your time?

_____

_____

What does a typical day look like?

_____

_____

FAMILY

My children and their current ages

_____

_____

My "grands" and "great grands" and their current ages

_____

_____

Others I'm close to (cousins, etc)

_____

_____

Pets

_____

_____

Thoughts

_____

_____

THE PRESENCE OF GOD IN MY LIFE

(Let's get specific)

Were you raised in a Christian home? Yes/No

Did you have a church family? Yes/No

How was that experience?

_____

_____

As a child, did you attend Sunday School, Bible Study, Awana, etc? Yes/No

Were you saved as a child? Yes/No

Were you baptized? Yes/No

Did you have a youth group? Yes/No

If you became a believer as a youth, how old were you? _____

When did you realize that your life would be different as a believer?

_____

Did you have an "epiphany moment?" Yes/No

What clinched it for you?

_____

_____

Did you ever ignore God or reject Him? Yes/No

When did you first feel the presence of God in your life? (you may or may not have been a "true" believer at this point)

_____

_____

Other "GOD moments" that you remember

_____

_____

I never remember a time without Him!

Now that's a tough one...

HOW I CAME TO KNOW GOD

(my testimony)

_____

_____

_____

_____

_____

_____

_____

_____

_____

_____

_____

_____

_____

_____

_____

_____

_____

_____

_____

"When I first met Jesus..."

VERY PRIVATE PAGE

Circle all the things that have happened or are happening to you...

I EXERCISE   VETERAN   MARRIED   AM SAVED   PREACHER'S KID   I SEW

PARENTS DIVORCED   I'M DIVORCED   UNEMPLOYED   HAD CAR ACCIDENT

I HAVE A DREAM JOB   MONEY PROBLEMS   I WAS HOMESCHOOLED   I FEEL PLAYFUL

HAD A MISCARRIAGE   HIGH SCHOOL DROPOUT   SINGLE MOM   LIKE TO DANCE   I HAVE OCD

OCD IN FAMILY   CHANGED SCHOOLS AS A KID   HAD AN ABORTION   COLLEGE GRAD

HAVE ONE CLOSE FRIEND   GAVE BIRTH   FEEL LONELY   ADDICTION   LOVE COFFEE

SINGLE MOM   HAVE PHYSICAL AILMENTS   AM A GRANDPARENT   LOVE TO WALK

EXPERIENCE DEPRESSION   DIFFICULT MARRIAGE   I HAVE REBELLIOUS CHILDREN   LOVE TO READ

EXPERIENCED CHURCH SPLIT   LOVE TO DO PUZZLES   DEATH OF FAMILY MEMBER   BETRAYAL

HAVE PHYSICAL LIMITATION/S   SOUGHT COUNSELING   TRAVELED OUTSIDE U.S.   DISABILITY

LOVE SHORT TRIPS   LOSS OF A PARENT   LOSS OF A SPOUSE   CONTEMPLATED SUICIDE

INVOLVED IN CHURCH   HAVE A PET   HAVE A SPECIAL NEEDS CHILD   BEEN CHEATED ON

BROKE COMMANDMENTS   LOVE BOARD GAMES   DON'T EXERCISE   LOVE TO GARDEN

I KEEP A JOURNAL   NO CLOSE FRIENDS   OVERWEIGHT   I HOMESCHOOL

I HAVE SPECIAL NEEDS   I DRAW   MENTAL HEALTH ISSUES   LIVE ALONE   DON'T GO TO CHURCH

I WRITE   HAVE MAJOR ILLNESS   LOVE DOING CRAFTS   I NEED MORE SLEEP

FAVORITE BIBLE VERSES

_____

_____

_____

_____

_____

_____

_____

_____

General Time Period Sheet

General Time Period Sheet

Decades Sheet

0-10	10-20	20-30	30-40	40-50	50-60	60-70+

AUTHOR EXAMPLE

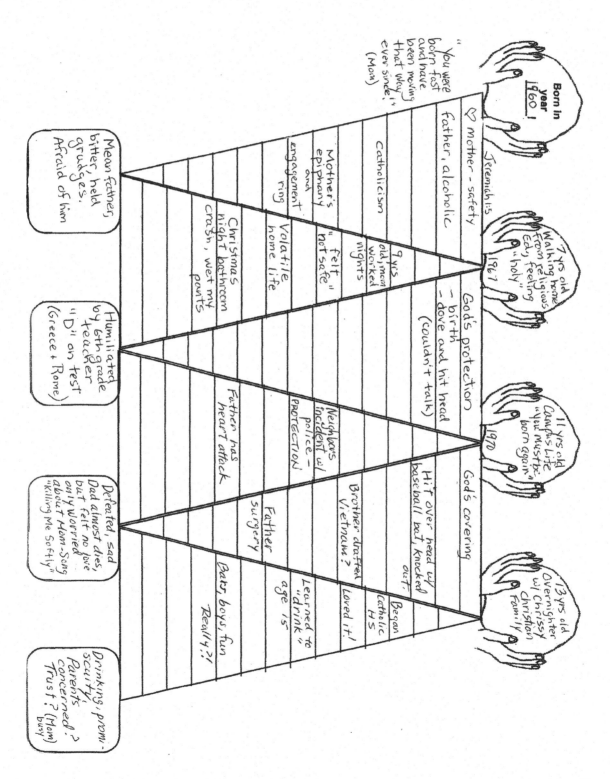

AUTHOR EXAMPLE

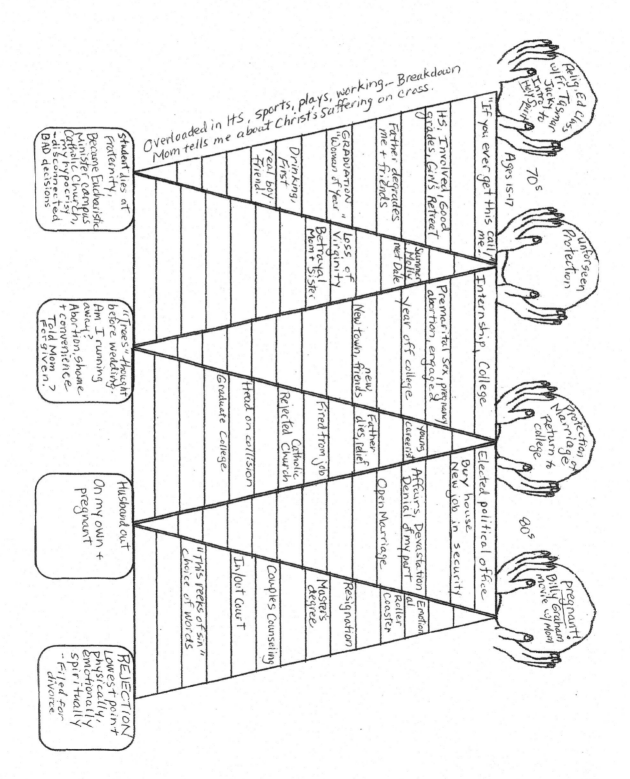

AUTHOR EXAMPLE

Dates:	Ebenezer:
1960	My birth, almost died God gave me a wonderful mommy
1967	Walking home, feeling "holy"
1970	Campus Life "You must be born again"
1972	experienced Christian home Chrissy
76/77	Mom's comfort HS overload Religious Ed Class – Jacky "How will I know?" Holy Spirit
76-86	Protection Worldly successes He would use later in life
Summer 1986	Billy Graham movie with Mom, prayed
1986	Curtis Born – prayed for him Infant Baptism
86-97	Provision Mom's help Mother gets saved but I didn't know
Fall 88	My dream from God: "Move away from sin, come follow me and sing my praises. I have just shown you a glimpse of my glory."
	SAVED! The reason I was born New chapter in my story!

Date	Ebenezer

Date	Ebenezer

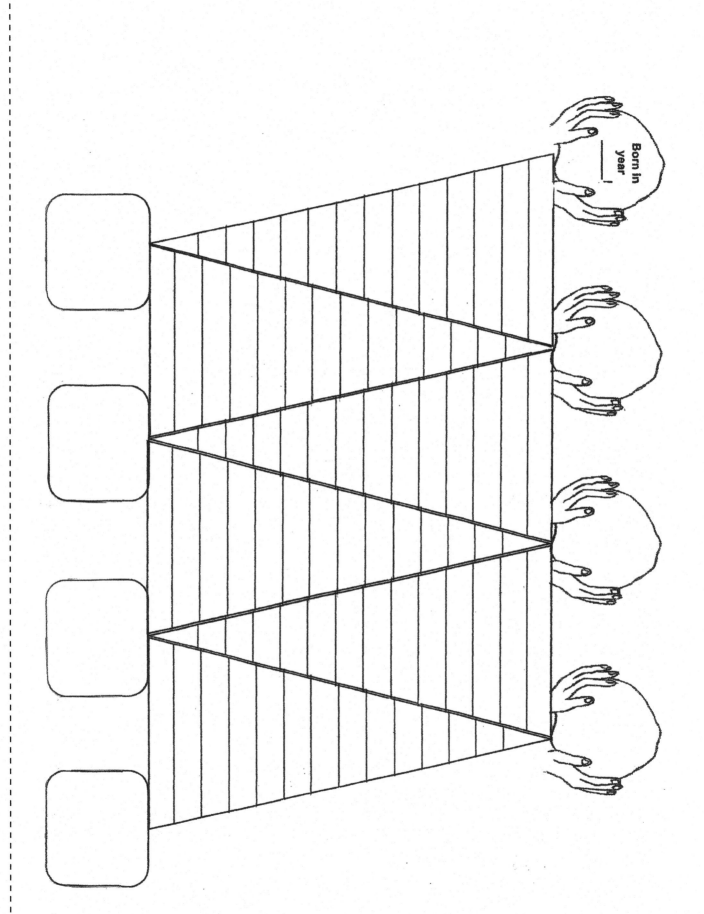

Born in
year
____

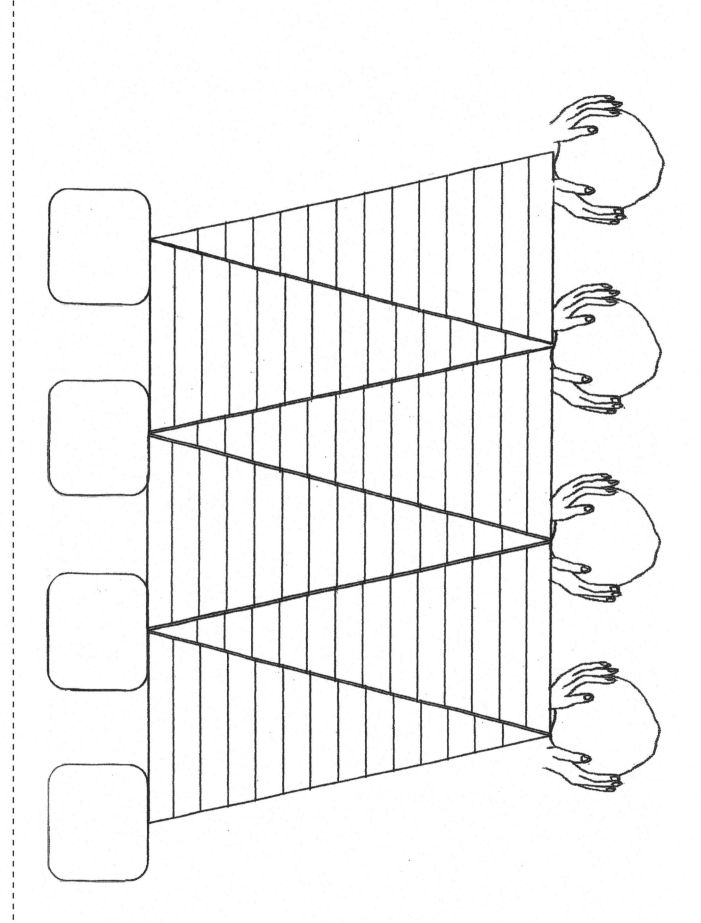

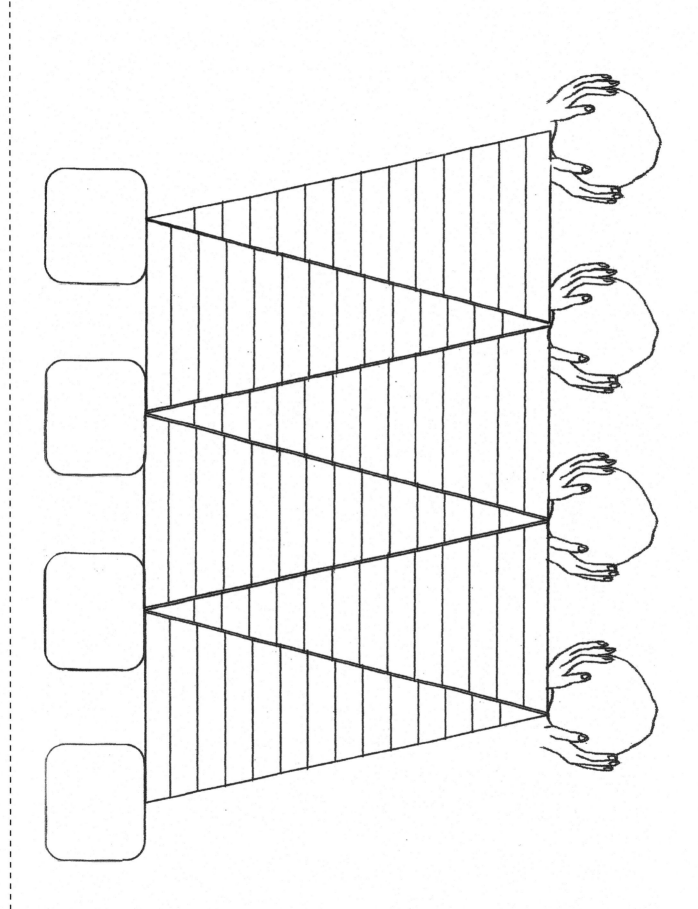

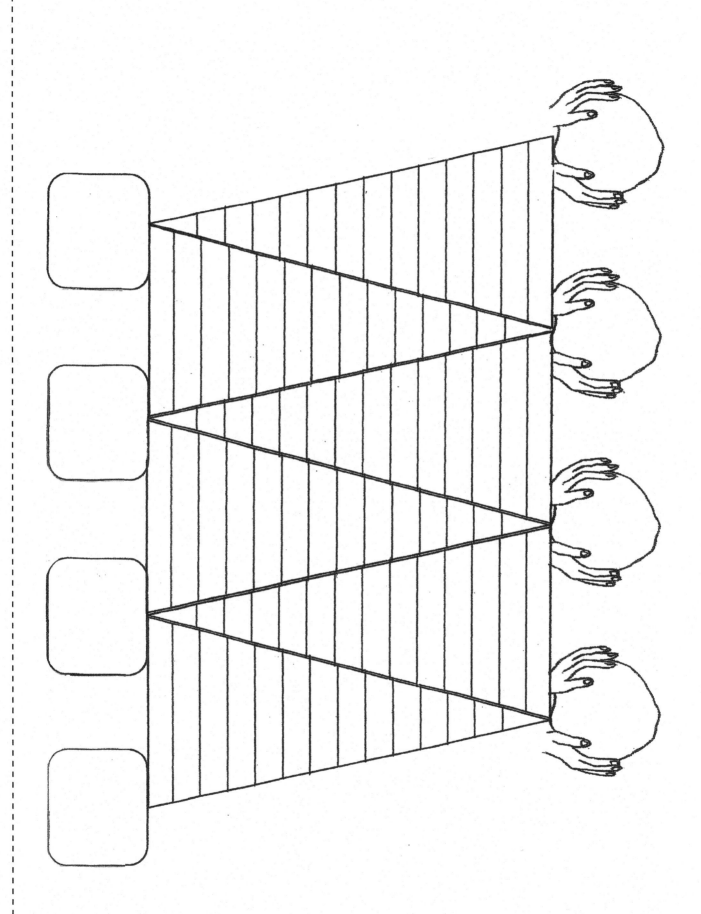

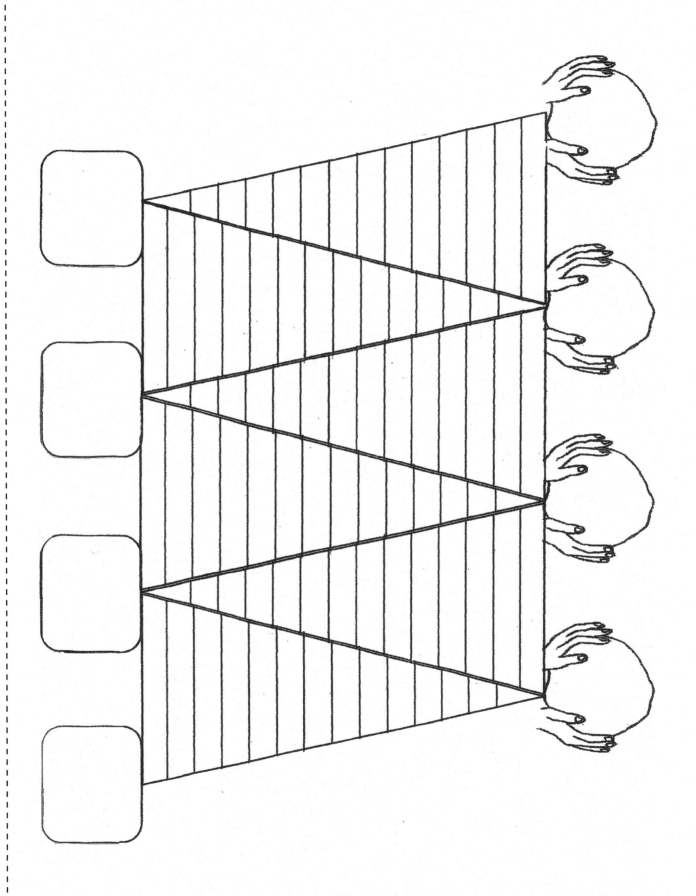

81

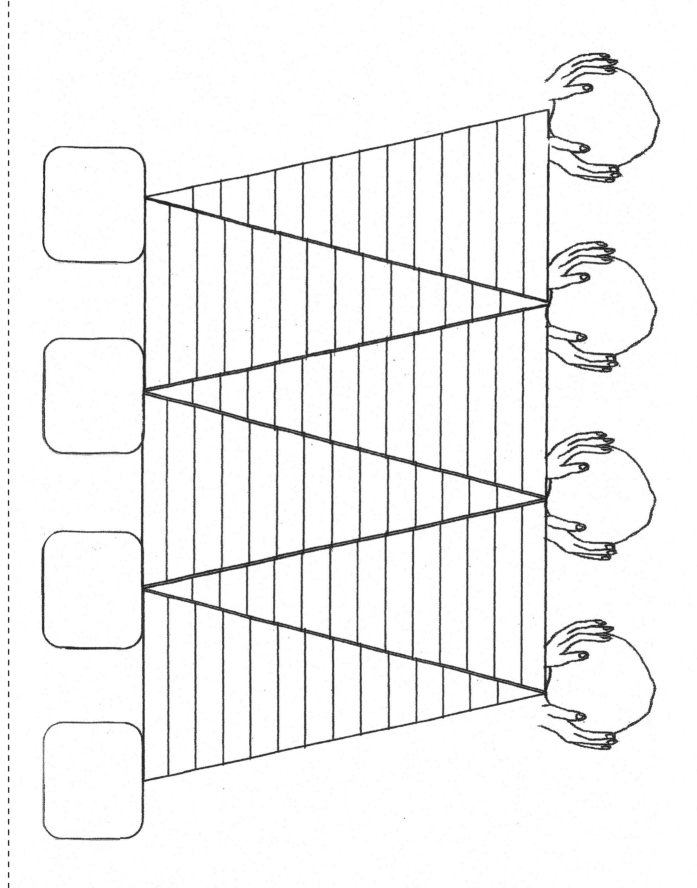

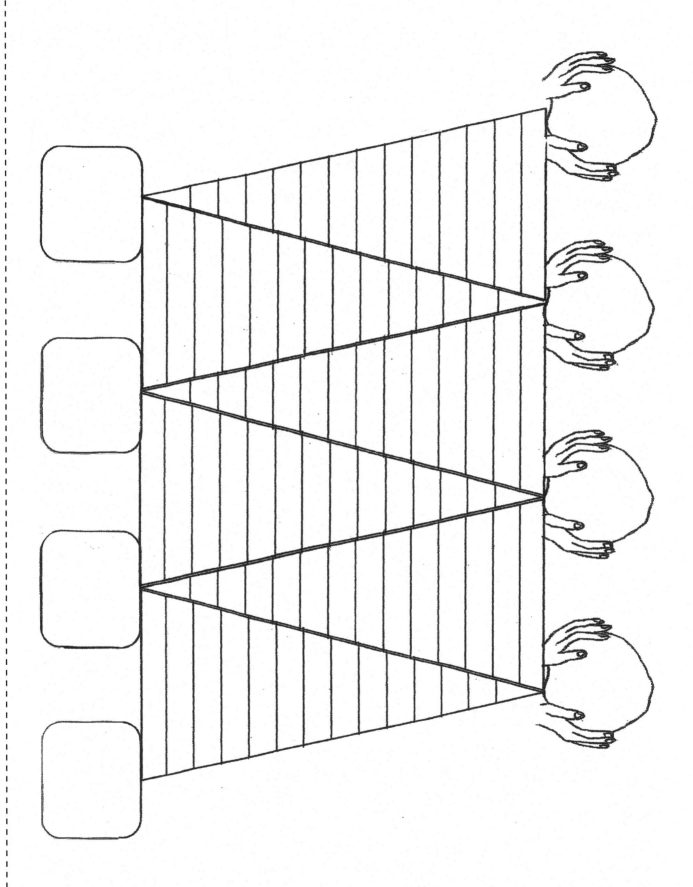

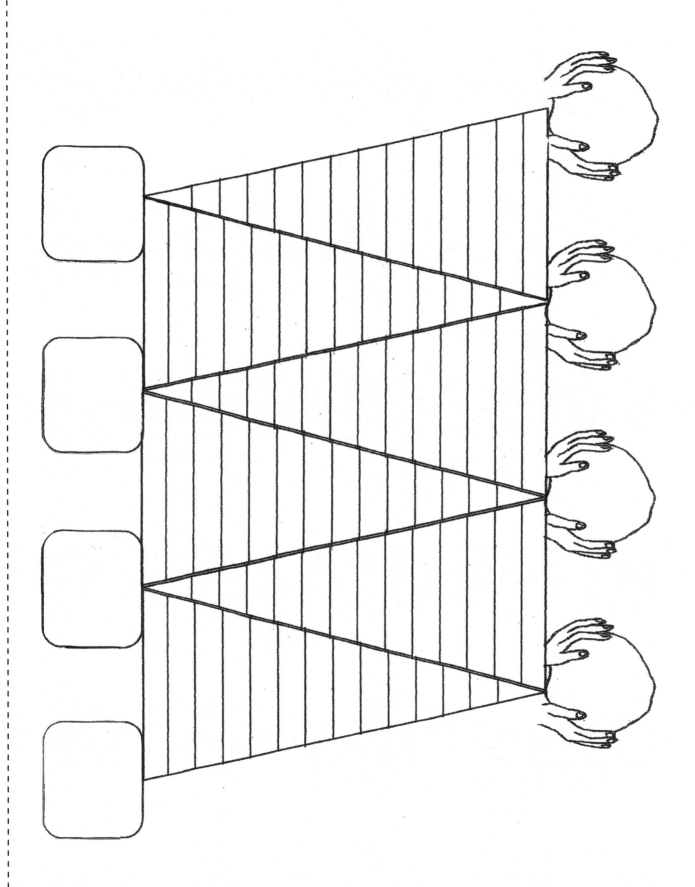

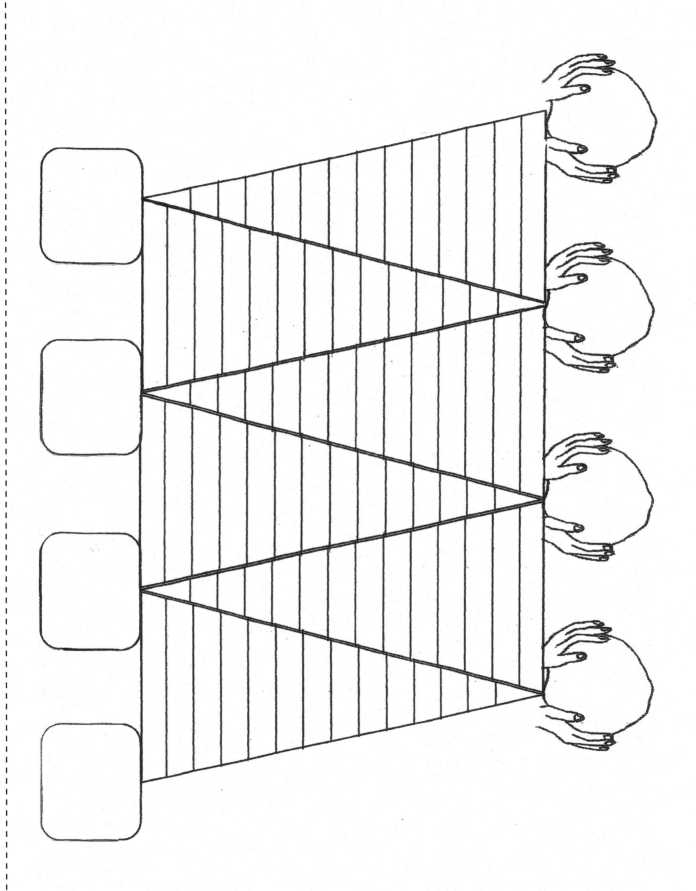

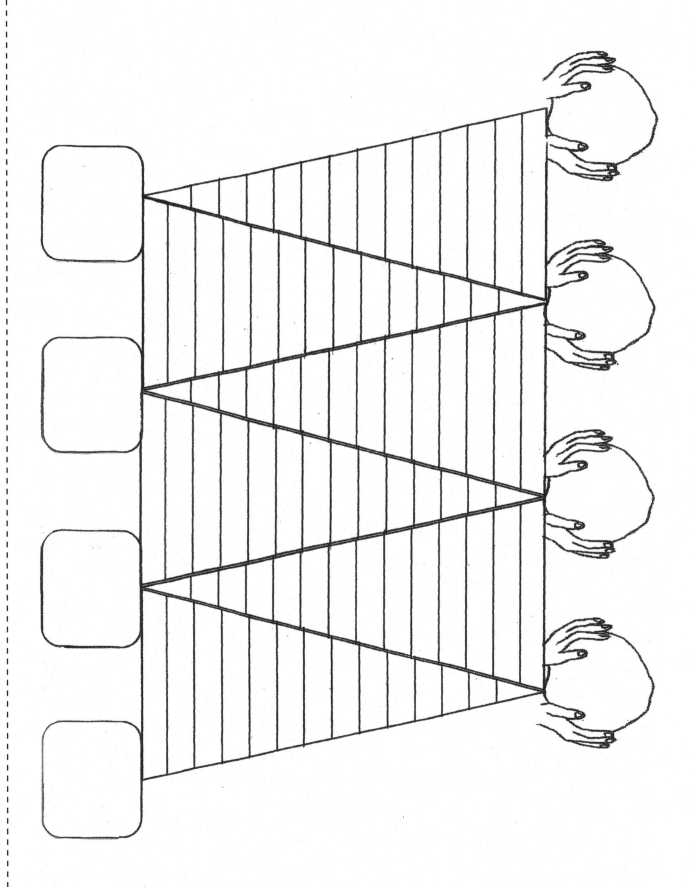

ACKNOWLEDGEMENTS

I have never written a book before. It took me 9 years and it was hard. Now I realize why the "Acknowledgements" are so important. I will never skip reading them again. Undoubtedly, this book was a calling from Jesus Christ and He led my every step. I slipped into "bit and bridle" mode quite a bit but He was relentless.

Thank you, Lord. I have learned to trust you more and I am really looking forward to adding to my map. And when I can't add anymore, I will be with you! You are exhilarating!

To my beloved mother, you will always be my best friend. Thank you for listening to the early memoir. When you would ask, "Can we read more today?" I thought my heart would burst. We will both have to wait and see how it ends. Mom, words could never…see you on the other side.

To my husband, thanks for listening even when your eyes were closing, and for all the encouragement over the course of this project. Your insight was invaluable. To my kids, I appreciate you taking my phone calls even when you were tired of hearing about "the book!" Daughter, you shoot from the hip and it always makes me pause and rethink. Thank you making forms and power point pages on the run. Son, you missed your calling, (I know, I know!) and I benefitted so much. It didn't go unnoticed that you would both just drop everything to help and spur me on. I know it must have been difficult at times to hear about my former life, but you guys were champs. To my "editors," and son, writer extraordinaire, you were all spot on and I so appreciate the time you gave me.

To a dear, longtime friend—I loved all the conversations about our writing projects and the sweet details of life. Thank you for the encouragement and publishing guidance. I miss you. To my pastor's wife and friend for her invitation to share our writing pieces together. I was scared to death, yet you inspired, challenged and believed in me when I didn't. This book would not be if it wasn't for you. To my friends and sisters who did lot of early work. You were sounding boards and advisors. When I was lost in the technological jungle, you took my hand. You told me my ideas and writing style were good! To my neighbors, you always listened and applauded my efforts. The little newspaper clippings on writing, reading and life always came at just the right time. Thanks for making life fun.

My pastor, you are a gifted teacher and shepherd. This book started during that sermon in which you unraveled the term "Ebenezer." Then, every New Year's Eve service you would explain to the congregation why looking back on our lives was useful. You reminded us to always give God the glory, and to keep going because God is in control. "He is God and we are not." And the promised suffering? It's only for "a little while." He will work it all for good. To the deacons at church, you trusted me with this whole mapping idea for our ladies' retreat without even asking to see the curriculum. Thank you for your support.

To all 27 women who went on the retreat using my unpublished draft—I was over the moon that you would trust me enough to even sign up! You were genuinely excited to see what "Raise Your Ebenezer" was all about. To all my sisters in Christ, just watching you delve into the Inspiration Pages and begin mapping was the blessing of a lifetime. You prayed, worked tirelessly and we all lost sleep. You were an inspiration to me in finishing the book. I love each and every one you.

Thank you to the anonymous donor, and the two others who helped finance the retreat. You didn't even blink an eye and were such cheerful givers! There were many women who just stepped up to help pull off our mapping adventure. Thanks for taking charge, making copies, playing music and presenting crafts. A couple of you tended to the little things, like suggesting we "run for cover" when the thunder started! We were thrown together in a little room with lots of food and lots of tears. Thank you all for being so vulnerable on that very tender night. To all the husbands and fathers for holding down the fort while we were away.

God, thanks for the rainbow over the lake in the morning. Immeasurably more, immeasurably more…

Dear Reader

Thank you for purchasing and reading my book. As a new author, I am extremely grateful and hope you found value in the process of mapping your life. Please consider telling your family and friends about it and leaving a review online. Your support and feedback are so appreciated. Please go to Amazon if you would like to leave a review and to share a little of your journey. NOTE: You do not need to purchase the book from Amazon in order to leave a review on this site.

Love,

Kit

Printed in the United States
by Baker & Taylor Publisher Services